Caring for a cat with kidney failure

by Dr Sarah Caney BVSc PhD DSAM(Feline) MRCVS, RCVS Specialist in Feline Medicine

About Cat Professional

Cat Professional was founded in 2007 by Dr Sarah Caney with the aims of providing cat owners and veterinary professionals with the highest quality information, advice, training and consultancy services.

Publications

Cat Professional is a leading provider of high quality publications on caring for cats with a variety of medical conditions. Written by international experts in their field, each book is written to be understood by cat owners and veterinary professionals. The books are available to buy through the website www.catprofessional.com as eBooks where they can be downloaded and read instantly. Alternatively they can be purchased as a softback via the website and specialist bookstores.

'Caring for a cat with kidney failure' is the first in a series of books published by Cat Professional. Forthcoming publications include:

- 'Caring for a blind cat' – June 2008
- 'Caring for a cat with lower urinary tract disease' – August 2008
- 'Caring for a hyperthyroid cat' – September 2008
- 'Caring for a diabetic cat' – November 2008

German and Japanese translations of each book will be made available.

A variety of free-to-download articles also feature on the Cat Professional website.

Advice, Training and Consultancy

Cat Professional is dedicated to improving the standards of cat care and in this capacity is a provider of Continuing Professional Development to veterinary surgeons and other professionals working with cats around the world.

Cat Professional also works closely with leading providers of cat products and foods providing training programmes, assisting with product literature and advising on product design and marketing.

Specialist feline medicine advice is available to veterinary professionals and cat owners world-wide. Details are available on the website.

About the author

Sarah is an internationally recognised veterinary specialist in feline medicine who has worked as a feline-only vet since 1994. She trained as a specialist at the University of Bristol, England and is one of only eight recognised specialists in feline medicine working within the UK. Sarah has written many articles for veterinarians and cat owners and works very closely with the UK cat charity, the Feline Advisory Bureau, FAB (www.fabcats.org). Her work with FAB includes chairing their feline expert panel which lobbies organisations for better cat care and, for example, treatments which are 'easy to give' to cats (we all know how difficult it can be to medicate a cat!). Sarah has written one veterinary textbook (Self-Assessment Colour Review of Feline Medicine) with another feline expert, Andy Sparkes and, as a clinician sees a mixture of first opinion and referral feline patients. She has been invited to lecture on feline medicine at veterinary conferences all over the world. Sarah lives in Scotland and has a very handsome, elderly tabby cat called Hobi (pictured below right).

About this book

This book has been written as an electronic book available for downloading or printing on demand. 10% of the profit from each book sale will be donated to the Feline Advisory Bureau (Registered Charity number 1117342, www.fabcats.org) to help continue the excellent work they do in educating everyone who works or lives with cats. If you have obtained this book free from a friend or another source I would encourage you to visit my website www.catprofessional.com to obtain a bona fide copy of your own.

Words in purple are contained in the glossary section at the end of the book.

Dedications and acknowledgements

I would like to thank my partner Brendan (whose idea writing this book was) for all of his support and guidance during the writing process.

Thanks also go to all of those colleagues, clients and friends for their advice on what should be included and, of course, to the cats pictured for all looking so gorgeous!

The pictures included in this book are the copyright of the author except for the one of Morgan at home, kindly included with the permission of her owner.

CONTENTS

Overall, in the UK, kidney failure is thought to affect 1% of patients registered to a veterinary practice at any one time. The frequency of kidney failure is much higher in older cats and is estimated to affect around 30% of cats over the age of 15 years.

This guide has been written to provide cat owners with the information they need to understand this complex condition and provide the best care for their cat. The author regularly lectures on this subject and the contents of this book reflect what she teaches to veterinary students, veterinary nurses, technicians and qualified veterinary surgeons around the world.

Receiving bad news: coping with the emotional side of receiving a diagnosis of kidney failure in your cat

Being told that your cat has kidney failure has probably come as a very nasty shock. You are likely to be on a roller-coaster of emotions with a lot of worry about your cat. This section will aim to reassure you as well as prepare you for what is to come.

My first advice is to stop, take a deep breath and try to remain calm. Take some time to understand and come to terms with the diagnosis and what it means for your cat. Don't rush any decisions. In most cases, all is not lost and there are lots of things that you can do to restore your cat's quality of life. Remember, you are likely to be suffering more than your cat!

What is wrong with my cat?

Firstly, a diagnosis of kidney failure is not necessarily a death sentence! Although it is a progressive disease, with appropriate care and commitment you can help your cat to live a happy life – often for many years. Even in those severely affected cats needing hospital treatment and intravenous fluids, recovery to a good quality of life is possible. Don't immediately assume that your cat's life is over. However, kidney failure is a very serious condition– and all cases vary in the level of care that they need. Your vet is in the best position to advise you on your own cat and what the future might hold – discuss your concerns with them. At the worst, if diagnosed in severe kidney failure, your vet might advise you that euthanasia (putting your cat to

sleep) is the kindest option rather than any treatment. Terrible though this is, this is only the case in the minority of cats with kidney failure.

A diagnosis of kidney failure means that your cat's kidneys are not working as effectively as they should be and this is why your cat has been feeling ill. Section 2 covers the scientific aspects of this condition in much greater detail – you can read about the causes of kidney disease, how vets diagnose the condition and how it can best be treated.

Could I have prevented this from happening – was it my fault?

Many owners will immediately panic that they could have done more to prevent the illness from developing or that, if only they had taken their cat to the vet sooner, things might be different. Although it is impossible to generalise and I cannot comment on your own cat's circumstances, I will say that in my experience the following statements are true:

- The overwhelming majority of cases of kidney failure are caused by medical conditions which are completely out of an owner's control i.e. your cat is not ill because of something you have done! There are a few very rare exceptions to this – one would include allowing your cat access to lily plants.

If your cat eats part of a lily plant then this can be very harmful to their kidneys and, in severe cases, can cause fatal kidney failure.

■ Although it is always advisable to take your cat to the vet as soon as you realise it is ill, in most situations a short delay is unlikely to have changed their chances of recovery. Again there are some exceptions to this but they are rare – for example

causes of sudden kidney problems like the example of eating lilies highlighted above. This can be a rapidly deteriorating condition and every second counts when it comes to treatment!

> **a diagnosis of kidney failure is not necessarily a death sentence**

Cats are masters of hiding illness and, in most circumstances, we only realise our cats are ill when things have deteriorated to a very severe extent. Most of the signs of illness that a cat shows are also vague – such as sleeping more and losing weight. These signs can be very gradual and hard to spot on a day to day basis. Don't punish yourself for not realising that your cat is ill – you are not alone!

What is the treatment for this disease?

Treatment consists of:

1. Treating the cause of the kidney failure (where this can be found) – for example bacterial infections can be treated with antibiotics.

2. Helping the cat to cope with reduced kidney function. Depending on the individual cat and the severity of their disease this includes feeding a special diet, drugs that help to reduce vomiting, drugs to help improve the appetite and so on.

Section 2 discusses this in greater detail – the treatment for kidney failure is complicated as normal kidneys perform many vital functions. In the first instance, your vet may suggest that your cat is admitted to their hospital for intravenous fluid therapy (putting your cat on a drip). This is an effective treatment for dehydration which is common in kidney failure patients and often provides a significant 'boost' to affected cats. In most cases, the cat will not need to stay on a drip for more than a couple of days after which it can return home for treatment with you.

Is my cat in pain?

Kidney failure certainly makes a cat feel unwell but it is not usually a painful condition. Your vet will be able to advise you whether or not your cat is in any pain or distress and what treatments are available to help this.

Is it fair to put my cat on lots of different medications – am I being cruel to treat it?

Not all cats with kidney failure need medication. Feeding a kidney prescription diet is usually the most important treatment. Further medication beyond this will depend on your cat and whether they need certain drugs. In some cases, cats with kidney failure do need lots of different medicines and the thought of giving these to your cat can be daunting. My advice, would be not to give up without trying therapy as:

- some cats are surprisingly easy to medicate
- some cats will eat treatments reliably in their food
- for those cats on multiple medications empty gelatine capsules obtained from a vet or pharmacist can be very helpful. Several medicines can be put into one empty gelatine capsule reducing medication into one easy dosage. This was very helpful for Morgan (the case illustrated in Section 3) and has meant that her medication takes only a few seconds every day and does not cause her any suffering or distress.

It may take some time for you, and your cat, to get used to all of the treatments your vet has suggested but as long as your cat is happy and coping, it is worthwhile persevering. Don't forget to discuss how treatment is going with your vet – if you are having problems, they may well have solutions or suggestions for you.

Also, remember that we are talking about your cat – no one knows your cat better than you and if you feel that the treatment suggested is not right, for whatever reason, then your vet should respect this.

I'm not sure I can cope with treating my cat – help!

Learning of a diagnosis of kidney failure is going to come as a shock and will take some time to get used to. Once you have had a chance to think things through, chat with friends/family and your vet, hopefully everything will seem clearer and less daunting.

You can only do your best when it comes to caring for your cat and it is not always possible to do everything you want. For example if you have severe arthritis and are unable to give your cat a pill this may affect the level of treatment you can provide. Likewise, if your cat is completely intolerant to the thought of being medicated, this may prevent you from giving some treatments to it. In many situations, there are other options available – for example trying to hide medications in food or asking your vet to give an injection of the drug. Please note injections are not available for every type of medicine. In any case, your vet should be able to talk you through the options and, together, you should be able to make a plan that you both feel comfortable with.

Is kidney failure life-threatening?

Yes – kidneys are essential body organs so any cat with kidney failure will have a reduced life expectancy. However, many cats with kidney failure can live with an excellent quality of life for years after the diagnosis is made, especially if they receive treatment for this condition. For example, cats with kidney failure that will eat a special prescription kidney failure diet, have a doubled life expectancy compared to those cats with kidney failure that will only eat normal cat food. This is discussed in more detail in Section 2.

What is kidney failure?

Kidney failure (also known as **renal** failure or **renal** insufficiency) is the term used when kidney function is no longer able to meet the body's demands.

Cats and humans are born with more kidney tissue than is needed – this is called a functional reserve. This is why healthy adult humans can safely donate a kidney to a friend or relative.

Clinical signs of kidney failure are not seen until at least two thirds of the functional kidney tissue has been lost. Unfortunately this makes it difficult to diagnose cats in the very early stages of kidney failure.

Kidney failure is sub-divided into acute and chronic kidney failure. In medical terminology, acute means sudden (occurring over a period of less than 24 hours) therefore **acute renal failure** (ARF) means a sudden loss of kidney function which can be caused by one or more of the following:

- Reduced blood supply to the kidneys (so called pre-**renal** ARF). Causes include heart failure and dehydration.

- Damage to the kidneys themselves (**renal** or intrinsic ARF). Causes include poisoning e.g. antifreeze (ethylene glycol), eating lilies.

- Failure of urine excretion due to a blockage in the **urethra** (tube from the bladder to the outside) or rupture of the bladder. This is called post-**renal** ARF.

Although many causes of ARF are fully treatable (and the kidney damage can be fully reversed), if severe and untreated, ARF can progress to chronic kidney (**renal**) failure (CRF). In medical terms, chronic means something which has been present for at least 2 weeks. Chronic kidney failure is considered to be a progressive condition – it will get worse with time – although the speed of progression is variable.

Many cats will be presented to their vets when in 'acute on chronic' kidney failure. This is the situation present when a cat in chronic kidney failure is presented in an acute crisis. The cat may have been coping, more or less, in chronic kidney failure for some time but for example becoming dehydrated has precipitated a sudden crisis. Cats in acute on chronic crises often benefit from being admitted to a veterinary hospital and placed on an intravenous drip for a day or two.

> **Chronic kidney failure is considered to be a progressive condition – it will get worse with time – although the speed of progression is variable**

What do normal kidneys do?

The kidneys are required for a great number of important functions in the body. Normal cats are born with two kidneys, a right and a left kidney, which are located in the abdomen.

Normal kidneys are vital for good health and have many important functions including:

- Excretion of waste products via the urine. This includes protein breakdown products such as urea and creatinine.

- Regulation of normal body water content (hydration balance)

- Regulation of levels of blood salts (e.g. sodium, potassium, calcium and phosphate)

- Regulation of body acidity levels

- Production and activation of a number of hormones and other substances (e.g. erythropoietin – a hormone which stimulates production of red blood cells by the bone marrow)

What causes kidney failure?

The causes of kidney disease can be divided into two main categories:

- Congenital (those present at the time of birth) such as:

  – Polycystic kidney disease. This is an inherited cause of kidney failure which is especially common in Persian and related breeds. Affected cats are born with small cysts (fluid filled structures) in their kidney tissue. As the cat gets older, the cysts enlarge and eventually these compromise kidney function by putting pressure on the normal cells. Kidney failure develops once two thirds of the kidney tissue has been lost – typically this is when the cat is around 4 years old. Approximately 40% of Persians around the world are estimated to be affected by this inherited disease.

  – Renal dysplasia (abnormal development of one or both kidneys)

  – Being born with only one kidney

- Acquired conditions i.e. the cat is born with normal kidneys but develops a problem in later life. These include:

  – Bacterial and viral infections

  – Inflammatory conditions

  – Toxin exposure e.g. ingesting antifreeze or lilies

– Traumatic injuries e.g. damage to the kidneys following a car accident

– Cancer e.g. lymphoma (a cancer of white blood cells), adenocarcinoma (a cancer of glandular tissues)

Analysis of a kidney **biopsy** from cats with chronic kidney failure often shows that they have **chronic interstitial nephritis** – this term is used to describe the terminal kidney disease (scarring etc) that occurs irrespective of the initiating cause of the kidney failure. Unfortunately this means that it is not usually possible to determine the cause of the kidney failure once it has progressed to this point and is one reason why kidney biopsies are not commonly recommended (see later section What other tests are helpful in cats with kidney failure?).

Kidney failure is usually seen as a consequence of an acquired disease and is most common in middle-aged and older cats. Some breeds of cat are more likely to suffer from kidney failure than others – these include Abyssinian, Maine Coon, Persian and Siamese cats. There is no difference in the frequency of males or females affected by kidney failure.

Can kidney disease be prevented?

Many owners will immediately worry that they could have done more to prevent the illness from developing or that if only they had taken their cat to the vet sooner, things might be different. The overwhelming majority of cases of kidney failure are caused by medical conditions which are completely out of an owner's control. There are a few very rare exceptions to this:

■ Poisonings – for example lilies, grapes, raisins and antifreeze, are known nephrotoxins (substances known to be harmful to the kidneys) when ingested

■ Certain drugs – some drugs are known to have the potential to cause kidney damage. Where these are needed in your cat, your vet should discuss the potential for side-effects with you. Examples include certain antibiotics (e.g. gentamicin), non-steroidal anti-**inflammatory** agents (e.g. meloxicam – UK trade name Metacam, carprofen – UK trade name Rimadyl, ketoprofen – UK trade name Ketofen). Side-effects can occur with all drugs and all of the drugs listed above can be invaluable in treating cats with a variety of problems. For example, the non-steroidal anti-**inflammatory** agents provide pain relief and have made an enormous difference to the quality of life of cats with short-term pain (e.g. following a road traffic accident or surgery) and more long-standing conditions (e.g. arthritis). Fortunately in most healthy cats these drugs do not cause any side-effects to the kidneys. Where a cat is known to have kidney disease, these drugs need to be avoided or used at a much lower dose to try and avoid side-effects. As always, your vet is the best person to advise you on the use of these drugs – whether or not your cat has kidney disease.

Although it is always advisable to take your cat to the vet as soon as you realise it is ill, in most situations a short delay is unlikely to have changed their chances of recovery. Again there are some exceptions to this but they are rare – for example cases of acute kidney failure.

Therefore, in the majority of cases, there is nothing that can be done to prevent chronic kidney failure from occurring and, unfortunately, by the time it is obvious that the cat has a problem, at least two thirds of the functional kidney tissue has been irreparably lost.

What are the signs of kidney failure?

The **clinical signs** of kidney failure vary between individual cats but commonly include (in order of approximate decreasing frequency):

Polydipsia – an excessive thirst – is one of the clinical signs of kidney failure although it can be seen with other medical conditions such as diabetes mellitus ('sugar diabetes').

- Weight loss

- Reduced appetite

- Dehydration

- Lethargy – appearing listless and more tired than usual

- Increased thirst (**polydipsia**)

- Increased urination (**polyuria**)

- **Systemic hypertension** (high blood pressure) – this can cause problems with vision (including blindness), collapse, fits, behavioural changes

- Vomiting

- Anaemia (low red blood cell count)

- Mouth ulcers – often associated with bad breath (halitosis)

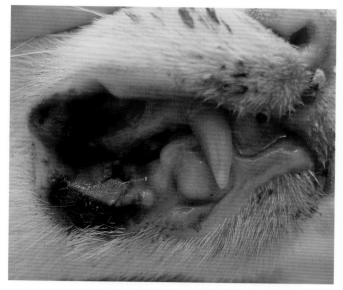

Mouth ulcers can be seen in very sick cats with kidney disease. In this patient, the margins of the lips in the left of the picture are swollen with areas that are greeny-brown in colour. This tissue is dead, infected, very painful and has an unpleasant smell.

How is kidney failure diagnosed?

Diagnosis is made through testing blood and urine samples. In patients with kidney failure, the kidneys will not have been excreting waste efficiently, so the blood will contain higher levels of waste products (such as urea and creatinine). Normal cats and dehydrated cats produce very concentrated (strong) urine – the ability to do this is lost as kidney failure worsens. Thus, cats with kidney failure have increased blood levels of urea and creatinine (referred to as 'azotaemia') and more dilute urine. It is essential to test both blood and urine samples since there are other causes of azotaemia (such as dehydration which is common in sick cats) which need to be ruled out.

It is common to have a combination of dehydration and kidney failure in the same patient (so called 'acute on chronic' kidney failure) and this can make the azotaemia even worse – in other words the urea and creatinine levels are higher than is just reflected by the cats kidney disease. If this is the case, then following correction of the dehydration (e.g. intravenous fluids – putting your cat on a drip) the urea and creatinine levels will fall. The level which they fall to is that reflected by the kidney failure.

Urine concentration is assessed using a refractometer which measures the urine specific gravity. Water has a specific gravity of 1.000. Normal cats usually produce urine with a specific gravity of at least 1.040. The lower the specific gravity, the more dilute the urine is. Kidney disease reduces a cat's ability to produce concentrated urine and the specific gravity falls to less than 1.035. In severe cases of kidney failure, the urine specific gravity can be as low as 1.015. It is important to bear in mind that other illnesses can affect the specific gravity mimicking kidney failure – these include:

- Diabetes mellitus (sugar diabetes): it is common for the urine specific gravity to be between 1.025 and 1.035. Sugar (glucose) is detected in the urine when a 'dipstick' test is done.

- Hyperthyroidism (overactive thyroid): it is common for affected cats to produce slightly dilute urine with a specific gravity of around 1.030.

- Liver disease: some cats with liver disease will produce more dilute urine (lower urine specific gravity).

- Diabetes insipidus: a rare disease in which affected cats produce very dilute urine (specific gravity less than 1.010).

Different laboratories have different reference ranges for blood test values such as urea and creatinine and, different countries use different units which further confuses matters. The two types of unit measurements used are:

- Conventional units: used by some countries including the USA

- SI units: used by most countries including the UK

The table below gives a guide to the reference range levels which are likely to be normal for where you live.

N.B. the reference range will vary slightly between laboratories so the following is just a rough guide:

Parameter	'Typical reference range' – Conventional units	'Typical reference range' – SI units
Urea	17 – 29 mg/dl	6 - 10 mmol/l
Creatinine	< 2 mg/dl	< 175 µmol/l
Phosphate	2.9 – 6.0 mg/dl	0.95 – 1.95 mmol/l
Potassium	4.0 – 5.0 mEq/l	4.0 – 5.0 mmol/l
Sodium	145 - 160 mEq/l	145 - 160 mmol/l
Calcium	8 - 10 mg/dl	2.0 – 2.5 mmol/l
Albumin	2.4 – 3.5 g/dl	24 - 35 g/l
Total protein	5.5 – 8.0 g/dl	55 - 80 g/l
Bicarbonate	18 - 24 mEq/l	18 - 24 mmol/l
Packed cell volume (PCV) or haematocrit	25 - 45 %	0.25 – 0.45
Haemoglobin (Hb)	0.8 – 1.5 g/dl	8 - 15 g/l

mg/dl – milligrams per decilitre   µmol/l – micromoles per litre   g/dl – grams per decilitre
mmol/l – millimoles per litre   mEq/l – milliequivalents per litre   g/l – grams per litre.

A **table** with conversion factors for transforming SI units to Conventional units (and vice versa) is contained in the Reference section (Section 5).

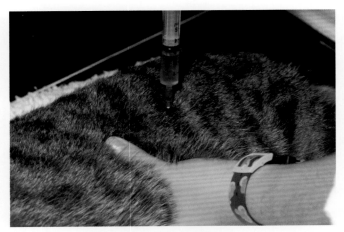

Cystocentesis is a commonly used technique to obtain a urine sample. A needle is passed through the skin and into the bladder from where urine is collected. This is a procedure which is well tolerated by cats and can be done with them fully conscious, gently restrained by a nurse.

Collection of blood and urine samples should not be a stressful event for a cat. Blood is most easily collected from the jugular vein which is the largest vein and is located in the cat's neck. Alternatively it can be collected from a cephalic vein which is a smaller vein, found on the front surface of the forelimbs. Urine samples can be collected in a variety of ways:

- **Cystocentesis**: this is the procedure by which urine is collected using a needle and syringe. The cat is gently held and the needle is passed through the skin of the tummy into the bladder. This is not a painful procedure and allows collection of a sterile (free from bacterial contamination) sample which is ideal for the tests needed.

- **Catheter samples**: urine can be collected using a catheter which is passed through the **urethra** (the tube from the outside of the cat to the bladder). Unfortunately this is not an appropriate technique for urine collection in most cats as it requires **sedation** (providing a state of calm and muscle relaxation using drugs) or **anaesthesia** (providing a state of unconsciousness, muscle relaxation and loss of pain sensation using certain drugs).

- **Free catch samples**: urine can be collected from an empty litter tray or one containing non-absorbent cat litter. Lots of different types of non-absorbant cat litter are available (e.g. Mikki, Katkor) or cheaper alternatives can be used (e.g. clean aquarium gravel, chopped up plastic bags). Once the cat has urinated, the

'Free catch' urine samples can be collected by using non-absorbent cat litter (Mikki® litter has been placed in this cat's litter tray). Once the cat has urinated the tray is tipped and a syringe or pipette used to collect a sample of urine for analysis.

urine can be collected using a syringe or pipette. It is important that the sample is collected as soon as possible after urination. Free catch samples are acceptable for initial assessment of kidney function. For example the **refractometer** test which determines the concentration of the urine is not affected by the method of collection. Free catch samples are not suitable for bacterial culture as they will be contaminated by bacteria in the litter tray and on the cat's paws.

Urine should be analysed as quickly as possible although many of the parameters that vets will be most interested in are not critically affected by storage for up to 24 hours. Urine tests include:

■ Specific gravity measured using a **refractometer**.

■ Urine dipstick to check for sugar (glucose) or other abnormalities.

■ Sediment examination: looking for cells, bacteria, crystals or other material in the urine sample under a microscope. For example this can help to diagnose a urinary tract infection.

■ Urine protein tests – for example the **urine protein to creatinine ratio** (referred to as the UPC or PCR test). This is a laboratory test which quantifies the severity of **proteinuria** (protein loss into the urine). Ratios greater than 0.4 are

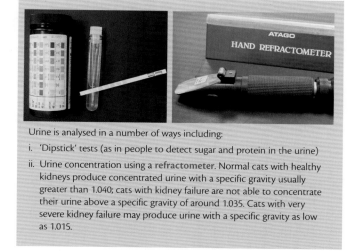

Urine is analysed in a number of ways including:

i. 'Dipstick' tests (as in people to detect sugar and protein in the urine)

ii. Urine concentration using a **refractometer**. Normal cats with healthy kidneys produce concentrated urine with a specific gravity usually greater than 1.040; cats with kidney failure are not able to concentrate their urine above a specific gravity of around 1.035. Cats with very severe kidney failure may produce urine with a specific gravity as low as 1.015.

currently considered to be abnormally high in cats with kidney failure and are thought to be an indication of ongoing damage to the kidneys.

■ Bacterial culture to see whether there is any evidence of infection. When a bacterial infection is diagnosed by the laboratory they will do a sensitivity test to identify which antibiotics are likely to be most effective in treating the infection. This is a test which takes a few days to perform.

What other tests are helpful in cats with kidney failure?

Once a diagnosis has been made, other blood tests (**haematology** and **biochemistry**) and urine tests will help to determine whether or not the cat is suffering from any other consequences of their kidney failure. These include:

- **Dehydration**: blood levels of salts, proteins and red blood cells can help to identify dehydration in affected patients. Dehydrated cats will usually be quiet and withdrawn.

- **Anaemia**: low levels of red blood cells can be detected using **haematology**. Anaemic cats will often be quiet and spend more time sleeping or resting than is normal for them. They may demonstrate an abnormal appetite (referred to as 'pica') where they eat cat litter or soil or lick concrete. You may notice that their gums are pale (for example when the cat yawns).

- **Altered blood salt levels**: most commonly in kidney failure are increased blood phosphate levels (**hyperphosphataemia**) and low blood potassium levels (**hypokalaemia**). Other blood salts which can be affected by kidney failure include sodium and calcium.

  - Cats with **hyperphosphataemia** may show **clinical signs** including loss of appetite, vomiting and depression.

  - Cats with **hypokalaemia** may have a poor appetite, be more quiet/withdrawn than normal and in severe cases show dramatic muscle weakness. This can be manifested as an inability to lift the head (see picture on **page 30**).

- Altered blood acidity – **acidosis**: the blood is more acidic than it should be. Affected cats are often very ill with no appetite and no energy and may vomit.

- **Proteinuria**: In mild to moderate cases, this might not be associated with any specific **clinical signs**. Cats with more severe or long-standing **proteinuria**, may develop abnormally low blood protein levels (**hypoproteinaemia**) which can cause the face, legs and skin of the tummy to appear puffy or swollen (due to **oedema** development). Development of fluid in the chest (**pleural fluid**) or tummy (**ascites**) can also be seen and this can cause, respectively, breathlessness and a swollen/enlarged abdomen.

- Bacterial urinary infection. Unfortunately, many cats with urinary infections do not show specific **clinical signs** (i.e. the infection is 'silent') and may only show vague **clinical signs** such as weight loss and lethargy. A small proportion of cats with urinary infections show **clinical signs** of **cystitis** including urgency to pass urine, passing small amounts of urine very frequently and passing bloody/smelly urine.

Dilation of the pupils (i) is one potential indication of blindness associated with high blood pressure as in this case. When a light is shone into the cat's eyes (ii), the pupils remain large and the retina can be seen (both of these findings are abnormal). Small areas of bleeding can also be seen in the cat's left eye – another consequence of her high blood pressure. Unfortunately the blindness was permanent in this cat.

It is important to identify and treat any of these additional problems, as it will help to make your cat feel as well as possible. It is also prudent to screen for other concurrent illnesses – it is not unusual to find that cats with kidney failure have more than one problem!

It is now known that a significant proportion of kidney failure patients (estimated to be at least 20 per cent) suffer from **systemic hypertension** (high blood pressure). **Systemic hypertension** is a serious condition that can cause blindness, seizures, heart problems and continued damage to the kidneys. Blood pressure can be measured in most practices. If facilities are not available to measure blood pressure, then your vet may refer you to another practice or to a specialist so that this test can be done. Examination of the eyes can be extremely helpful when checking for signs of hypertension – your vet may be able to see abnormalities such as bleeding into the eye or retinal detachment (where the retina – the 'seeing' layer of tissue at the back of the eye – lifts off). **Systemic hypertension** can cause permanent blindness if left untreated.

In some patients, additional tests such as x-rays and ultrasound of the kidneys may be useful for diagnosis. For example, polycystic kidney disease can be diagnosed by ultrasound and most kidney stones will be visible on an x-ray. Ultrasound can usually be performed with the cat fully conscious but x-rays usually require **sedation** or **anaesthesia**.

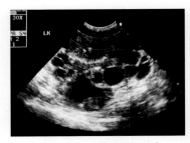

Ultrasound is a very effective way of diagnosing conditions like polycystic kidney disease. In this patient, many black circles corresponding to fluid-filled cysts can be seen on the scan picture of a cat's kidney.

In some cases, it is helpful to collect a kidney **biopsy** to determine the precise nature of the kidney disease. A **biopsy** involves collection and laboratory analysis of a sample of tissue such as the kidney. Biopsies can be collected in three main ways:

Blood pressure is most accurately measured using a Doppler machine and is a procedure which is very well tolerated by fully conscious cats. A cuff attached to a pressure gauge (called a sphygmomanometer) is placed on a forelimb or the tail; a separate sensor (the Doppler probe) is used to detect the pulse below the cuff. The cuff is inflated until the pulse signal disappears and then deflated slowly. The systolic blood pressure (higher of the two blood pressure readings we get when our own blood pressure is measured) is the pressure at which the pulse is first detectable.

1. Fine needle aspirate (FNA): the technique by which a sample of cells is sucked out of the kidney using a needle inserted through the skin. This procedure is relatively safe ('non-invasive') but often will not give enough information as to the precise nature of the disease.

2. Needle core **biopsy**: the technique by which a cylinder of tissue is obtained using a special needle inserted through the skin (under the guidance of ultrasound). This provides more tissue than an FNA but even so may not provide sufficient tissue to always make an accurate diagnosis.

3. Wedge **biopsy**: the technique by which a wedge of tissue is removed from the kidney via abdominal surgery. This provides

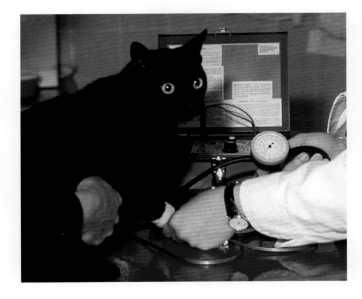

the best sample of tissue for a **pathologist** to examine but involves general **anaesthesia** (deep **sedation** can be sufficient for the other two techniques) and the associated surgical and anaesthetic risks.

In general, biopsies are not commonly performed as:

- In most cats with kidney disease, the **biopsy** results will not affect the treatment that the cat needs.

- It is a procedure which carries a high risk of bleeding which can be fatal in some cases.

- The procedure requires **sedation** or **anaesthesia** which can be risky in some patients with kidney failure.

- The **biopsy** procedure can worsen kidney disease by causing scarring in the kidney.

Examples of situations where a **biopsy** is indicated would include:

- Some cancers e.g. lymphoma – a cancer which responds to drug treatment

- Cats with severe **proteinuria**

- Young cats with kidney failure

In these situations precise knowledge of the nature of disease can make a difference to the treatment offered and long-term outlook for the affected cat.

What is staging of kidney disease and what does this mean?

The International Renal Interest Society (IRIS: **www.iris-kidney.com**) has devised a staging system for categorising the severity of kidney disease based on laboratory results (blood and urine) and blood pressure. It is important to use urea and creatinine values obtained after the cat has been re-hydrated since – as stated earlier – dehydration increases urea and creatinine levels and may give a false impression that the kidney disease is worse than it actually is. IRIS provides support and advice to veterinary surgeons regarding when to institute different treatments.

How is kidney failure treated?

Treatment varies greatly according to the individual's needs. In the vast majority of cases, treatment proves effective in stabilising a patient and helping to giving them a good quality of life for months or years. Although the damaged kidneys will not recover and chronic kidney disease will get progressively worse

Treatment can make an enormous difference to the cat's quality and length of life

with time, treatment can make an enormous difference to the cat's quality and length of life.

In general, treatment falls into the following categories:

Treatment of the underlying cause

Where possible, the cause of the kidney disease should be identified and treated. Unfortunately, in the majority of cases, a cause cannot be identified. An example of a treatable cause of kidney disease is a bacterial infection. Depending on the severity of the damage caused by the infection, treatment with antibiotics may be able to completely reverse the kidney failure (acute kidney failure situations). However, if the disease has been present for some time (weeks or months) there is a high chance of permanent damage which cannot be reversed by the antibiotics. In this situation, the antibiotics are only effective in stopping further worsening of disease. Even in these cases, treatment is worthwhile and can restore the cat's quality of life and allow the cat to be stabilised for months or years.

A range of commercially available kidney diets (in dry and wet forms) exist to cater for all tastes.

Specific dietary therapy (kidney diets) have been shown to dramatically improve the quality of life and survival (length of life) of cats with chronic renal failure.

Dietary management

Specific dietary therapy (kidney diets) have been shown to dramatically improve the quality of life and survival (length of life) of cats with chronic renal failure. There are many different types of kidney diets available via veterinary surgeons – in the UK these include:

- Hill's k/d available as dry food, pâté formulation tins and minced formulation (a very soft food) tins. Both tins are chicken flavour.

- Royal Canin Renal available as dry food and pouches (chicken and beef flavours).

- Eukanuba Renal available as dry food and tins.

- VetXX Specific available as a wet food in a foil tray.

Home-prepared diets are not recommended as it is very difficult to ensure that these remain balanced and safe for long-term use.

Many of the constituents required for preparation of balanced home-prepared diets are not available in the UK following BSE (bovine spongiform encephalopathy) restrictions.

Commercially made kidney diets are modified in several different ways:

- Restricted levels of high quality protein which limits the amount of protein breakdown waste products for the ailing kidneys to excrete.

- Restricted levels of phosphate since cats with kidney failure have a tendency to retain excess amounts of this which can contribute to their feeling unwell.

- Increased amounts of potassium and B vitamins which kidney failure cats are vulnerable to losing in their urine. B vitamin deficiency can cause a loss of appetite so it is important to avoid/treat this in cats with kidney failure.

- Increased numbers of calories which helps kidney failure cats with a poor appetite to maintain a normal body weight.

- Reduced levels of sodium which may help to reduce the risk of systemic hypertension from developing.

Kidney diets should be introduced gradually to your cat (e.g. over a period of a few days or weeks) and they should not be offered if your cat is unwell (e.g. vomiting) as your cat might associate the new diet with feeling unwell and refuse to eat the diet again in

Hand feeding is a useful nursing technique which can be done in both hospitalised and home-cared for patients to help encourage eating. Warming the food slightly, talking to the cat and stroking it can also help.

the future. Tactics which help to encourage acceptance of the new diet include:

- Offering a small amount of food by hand.

- Warming the food gently (so that it is warmer than room temperature but a little cooler than body temperature).

■ Adding liquid to the diet to make it softer.

■ Grooming and sitting with your cat whilst feeding it.

If, in spite of following all of these tactics, your cat refuses to eat the kidney diet then don't despair. There is a range of treatments which can be used to help make a normal cat food into one more like a kidney diet – for example, where needed, by adding extra potassium or phosphate binders (which stick to phosphate in the food and stop it from being absorbed). More information on phosphate binders and potassium is in the section 'treatment of specific complications'.

A senior diet is better than normal cat food (as these generally have lower levels of protein and phosphate) but *some* food is always better than *no* food – depending on your cat, you may need to compromise. Again, don't punish yourself if you find yourself in this situation – you can only try your best!

Cats with kidney failure often have a poor appetite – the use of appetite stimulants such as the anti-histamine cyproheptadine (trade name Periactin), mirtazapine (trade name Zispin) or anabolic steroids (e.g. nandrolone) can be helpful.

In some cases, placing a feeding tube into the oesophagus or stomach is helpful to provide extra food. Although anaesthesia and a short period of post-operative hospitalisation are required to place the tube, once in place these can be used for prolonged periods to administer food, liquids and medicines. Feeding tubes

'Skin tenting' is one indication of dehydration. To do this test, a bit of skin – for example the skin of the scruff – is gently lifted up and then let go. In healthy cats, the skin immediately returns to its normal position; in dehydrated cats the skin is slow to return to its normal position or stays standing up ('tented').

are not appropriate for all patients – they should be reserved for those that are otherwise well but where other tactics to increase appetite have failed.

Treatment of dehydration

Dehydrated cats will usually be quiet and withdrawn. A vet may be able to diagnose dehydration on a physical examination of your cat. Testing blood levels of salts, proteins and red blood cells can also help to identify dehydration in affected patients.

In the early stages following a diagnosis, your vet may suggest that your cat is admitted to the hospital for intravenous fluid therapy – putting your cat on a drip. This can be very effective in improving your cat's condition and giving it a boost before it

Severely dehydrated cats can be hospitalised and treated using intravenous fluids (fluid given by a drip into a vein).

i. This involves placing a catheter (a tube) into the vein in the front leg. Drip tubing is attached to this.

ii. The fluid can be pumped into the cat using special pumps (such as the syringe pump shown in this picture) or with the aid of gravity.

returns home for more long-term treatment. Intravenous fluid therapy is not something which should be viewed uniformly as a 'bad sign' – many cats will stabilise with this therapy and go on to do very well with standard treatment for their kidney failure at home.

Encouraging cats to drink and maintain normal hydration is very helpful; moist diets (i.e. canned or pouches) are preferable to dry ones. Some cats prefer eating the dry food and refuse moist diets – this is not necessarily a problem as long as the cat is encouraged to drink plenty. Some of these cats will eat dry food to which water has been added so this is worth a try.

Tips for encouraging your cat to drink more include:

- Ensuring that water supplies are always easily accessible to your cat – for example on every floor of the house and never too far away from where your cat may be sitting or sleeping.

- Experimenting with different water bowls – some cats prefer to drink out of tall jugs or glasses rather than bowls. Cats do not usually like their whiskers to touch the side of their food or water bowl so the water should be filled to the top or the bowl should be wide in diameter.

- Water fountains can be helpful in encouraging some cats to drink more. (e.g. Drinkwell pet fountain available from many suppliers including amazon.co.uk).

It is important to ensure that plenty of water is available to cats with kidney failure as they have increased needs compared to healthy cats. Some cats prefer drinking from interesting receptacles such as this cat who likes to drink from a jug.

- Offering flavoured water (see below).

- Experimenting with different types of water – e.g. tap water, mineral water to see if your cat prefers water from different sources.

- Adding water to your cat's food (whether it is wet or dry) – some cats will tolerate a food that resembles soup!

- If your cat has a feeding tube in place then extra fluid can also be given by this route.

Offering flavoured water may encourage your cat to drink more but it must not be a salty liquid as this can increase the risk of **systemic hypertension**. Examples of ways to do this include:

- Poaching chicken or fish in unsalted water and offering the liquid to your cat as a drink (this can also be frozen and therefore used over a period of time).

- Offering juice from a drained can of tuna/salmon in springwater (not brine) or frozen cooked prawns.

- Liquidising fish or prawns in water to create a fishy broth. Again this can be frozen for future use. Some owners find freezing the liquid in ice cube trays helpful. A cube of frozen broth added to a bowl of water may be enough to stimulate drinking.

- Water flavourers are available in some countries and may help cats to drink more.

Some cats may require repeated hospitalisation for intravenous fluid therapy (placing on a drip) to treat dehydration. In these patients, home treatment with subcutaneous fluids (SubQ fluids, administration of fluids under the skin using a needle) can be very helpful to prevent dehydration and hence future hospitalisation. Giving subcutaneous fluids is straightforward in the majority of cases although you will need training from your vet or vet nurse in how to do this. A very useful guide for this technique, written by Dr Andy Sparkes (another UK feline specialist) is available on my website www.catprofessional.com.

Subcutaneous fluid therapy is not needed in all cats with kidney failure – in fact, it is helpful in only a small proportion of cases: cats suffering from repeated bouts of dehydration. In other cats with kidney failure, giving subcutaneous fluids (i.e. fluids extra to their requirements) can be harmful by putting an increased strain on their kidneys and risking overdose with the salts present in the fluids given. Your vet will be able to advise you as to whether your cat is a suitable patient for this therapy. In general, cats needing subcutaneous fluid therapy have one or more of the following in common:

- Their kidney failure is quite advanced (Stage 3 or 4 on the Iris scheme: www.iris-kidney.com and producing very dilute urine – urine specific gravity lower than 1.030).

- They will only eat dry diets – dehydration is likely since they generally are not good at drinking as much as they need to.

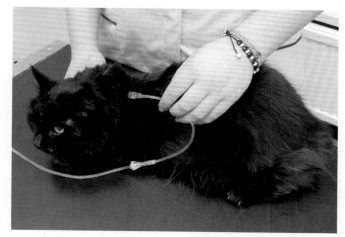

This patient is dehydrated and is receiving subcutaneous fluids (fluid given under the skin). This is a technique which can be done in the hospital. In those patients which are frequently becoming dehydrated, home subcutaneous fluid therapy can be done by the cat's owner following training and advice from a veterinary surgeon.

- They are not good at drinking very much (please note: it is normal for cats to not drink very much but when they have severe kidney failure this changes and they need to drink a lot to stay hydrated).

- They have suffered from dehydration in the past – for example needing hospitalisation and intravenous fluid therapy.

Subcutaneous fluid therapy is a fairly new therapy in some countries so it may not be something that all vets are familiar with. If your vet is not familiar with this therapy then they should find this book and information on my website helpful.

Treatment of specific complications

Some cats may have additional problems that need to be treated. Common problems include:

- **Hypokalaemia** (low blood potassium levels): Even with extra potassium provided in the special kidney diet, some cats will need additional potassium supplied as a liquid, powder or tablet. In the UK examples of potassium supplements are Tumil K (available as a tablet or as a powder which can be added to the food), Kaminox (a liquid supplement also containing B vitamins and iron, known in the USA as 'Amino B + K'). **Hypokalaemia** is diagnosed by measuring blood levels of potassium. Affected cats may have a poor appetite, be more quiet/withdrawn than normal and in severe cases show dramatic muscle weakness. This can be manifested as an inability to lift the head. If very severe, **hypokalaemia** can worsen kidney function. Fortunately, once corrected (i.e. potassium levels returned to normal) the kidney function improves. Severe **hypokalaemia** is sometimes best managed by hospitalising your cat and putting it on a high-potassium intravenous drip.

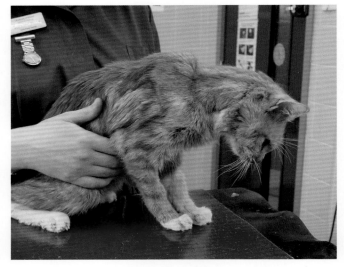

This is an example of ventroflexion of the neck: severe muscle weakness (so much so that this cat cannot lift his head) is present as a result of severe hypokalaemia (abnormally low blood potassium levels).

- **Hyperphosphataemia**: Cats that do not respond to dietary therapy or will not eat the prescription kidney failure diet will need to be prescribed drugs that limit the phosphate absorbed by the bowel. Phosphate binders are typically powders that need to be added to food before this is offered to the cat. Phosphate in the diet is bound by the drug, preventing its absorption by the bowel. Examples of phosphate binders

Remember to consult your vet for advice on what treatments your cat needs – not all treatments are needed (or will help) all cats. Never change your cat's treatment without discussing things with your vet otherwise this can cause problems.

available in the UK include aluminium hydroxide (e.g. trade name Alu Caps) and calcium containing compounds (e.g. trade name Ipakitine, Epakitin in the US). Hyperphosphataemia is diagnosed by measuring blood levels of phosphate. Cats with hyperphosphataemia may show clinical signs including loss of appetite, vomiting and depression.

■ Systemic hypertension: This is diagnosed by measuring the cat's blood pressure – facilities to do this are now present in most veterinary practices. Examination of the eyes can also be helpful in identifying clinical signs resulting from high blood pressure (e.g. bleeding into the eye). Affected cats can show a range of clinical signs including problems with vision (including blindness), collapse, fits and behavioural changes (e.g. pacing aimlessly, showing signs of dementia).

Sudden blindness is an emergency – prompt treatment can be successful in returning some vision although, sadly, many cats will remain blind for the rest of their life. It is currently recommended that systolic blood pressure (the higher of the two blood pressure readings) is kept below 170 mmHg (mmHg is the abbreviation for millimetres of mercury) in cats with kidney disease. Readings persistently above 180-190 mmHg risk potentially permanent organ damage. The most helpful drugs for treating high blood pressure are amlodipine (a human drug manufactured by Pfizer as Istin, Norvasc in the US) and ACE inhibitors such as benazepril (the trade name of the veterinary preparation is Fortekor).

■ Nausea and vomiting: sickness and vomiting has many causes in the kidney failure patient – these include:

– Severe azotaemia – best helped by feeding a low protein diet

– Hyperphosphataemia – helped by feeding a low phosphate diet and/or adding phosphate binders (substances which stick to phosphate in the food and stop it from being absorbed by the bowel)

– Acidosis – helped by feeding a prescription kidney diet and/or treating with sodium bicarbonate (not needed in all cats)

– Stomach ulcers – antacids and substances which soothe the lining of the stomach and help healing (known as

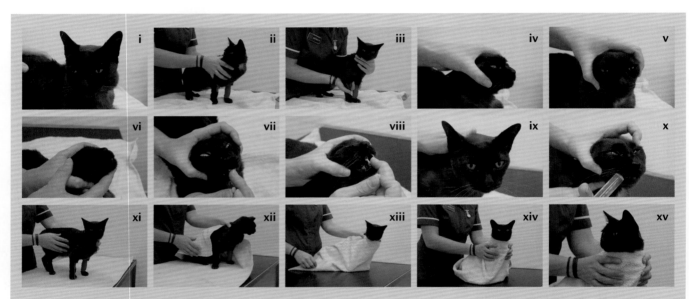

Medicating cats with pills or tablets

(i) try and ensure that your cat remains calm and relaxed; (ii) and (iii) the person restraining the cat gently holds the front legs so that they cannot come up and prevent pills being given or scratch you; (iv) and (v) make your forefingers and thumb into an arch shape and place this over the angle of the jaw holding the bony angle of the jaw firmly (this should not hurt your cat at all); (vi) tip your cat's head back gently so that the nose points to the ceiling; (vii) holding the pill between your thumb and forefinger gently open the jaw using your third finger; (viii) place the pill as far to the back of the mouth as possible; (ix) release your cat's head and allow them to swallow naturally, (x) syringe a small amount of water after giving the pill or allow your cat to have something to eat. (xi)–(xv) If your cat is very wriggly then placing them between your legs whilst you kneel on the floor or wrapping in a towel can help.

mucosal protectants) can be very useful. A wide variety of (mostly human) drugs are available for this and include sucralfate – a mucosal protectant (trade name Antepsin), and acid blockers such as ranitidine (a human drug, trade name Zantac) and famotidine (a human drug, trade name Pepcid).

Anti-sickness drugs such as mirtazapine (a human drug, trade name Zispin) and ondansetron (a human drug, trade name Zofran) can also be helpful in some cats.

■ **Anaemia**: Anaemic cats will often be quiet and spend more time sleeping or resting than is normal for them. You may notice that their gums are pale (for example when the cat yawns). Some anaemic cats will show an abnormal appetite – for example eating cat litter, soil or licking concrete. This abnormal appetite is called 'pica'. Anaemia is most accurately diagnosed by a blood test (**haematology**) which shows low levels of red blood cells. There are several causes of **anaemia** in cats with kidney failure. These include:

– Poor survival of red cells: red blood cells do not live as long as normal in cats with kidney failure. Unfortunately there is little that can actively be done to treat this. A mild **anaemia** is therefore quite common in cats with advanced kidney failure. Cats are very good at adapting to **anaemia** and adjusting their activity levels accordingly (i.e. spending more time resting).

Anaemia (a lack of red blood cells) is one of the possible complications of kidney failure and can make the nose (if non-pigmented) appear pale, as in this case.

– Iron deficiency: affected cats may benefit from iron supplementation by tablet or injection. Iron levels can be assessed by a blood test (iron and ferritin tests).

– **Erythropoietin** deficiency: **erythropoietin** is a hormone produced by the kidneys which stimulates production of red blood cells by the bone marrow. Levels of production can fall in cats with kidney failure and supplementation (with a synthetic human **erythropoietin**) can be helpful in some of these cats. Unfortunately there are some side-effects of this treatment – high blood pressure is one but most importantly the treatment may not work for very long as your cat's body may recognise the **erythropoietin** as a foreign protein and block it from working. In some cases this can make the **anaemia** worse than it was before treatment was started. As always, this is a treatment that should be discussed carefully with your vet.

– Stomach ulcers: these can cause blood loss into the bowel leading to **anaemia**. Drugs which help to soothe the bowel and prevent ulcers from forming can be helpful in some cats – examples include H2-blockers such as ranitidine (a human drug, trade name Zantac), famotidine (a human drug, trade name Pepcid) and drugs which help to protect the surface of the bowel such as sucralfate (trade name Antepsin).

Anabolic steroid treatments can also be given to try and stimulate the bone marrow to produce more red blood cells. This is quite a controversial treatment and probably not very effective.

If the **anaemia** is severe then a short-term treatment option would be a blood transfusion. Unfortunately this treatment only lasts for a few weeks (at the most) but it can be helpful in buying some time whilst other treatments (such as ulcer treatments) are taking effect. Blood transfusion is not an insignificant treatment – and donor cats are not always available – so it requires careful discussion with your vet.

- Altered blood acidity – **acidosis**: this is the situation when the blood is more acidic than it should be. Affected cats are often very ill with no appetite and no energy and may vomit. Prescription kidney diets can be very effective in preventing **acidosis** from developing. Some cats benefit from additional treatment – for example using sodium bicarbonate to normalise the blood acidity.

- **Proteinuria**: In mild to moderate cases, this might not be associated with any specific **clinical signs**. Cats with more severe or long-standing **proteinuria** may develop abnormally low blood protein levels (**hypoproteinaemia**) which can cause the face, legs and skin of the tummy to appear puffy or swollen (due to **oedema** development). **Pleural fluid** or **ascites** can also be seen and this can cause, respectively, breathlessness and a swollen/enlarged abdomen. Currently, the best known treatment for **proteinuria** is an ACE inhibitor such as benazepril (trade name Fortekor) – see later section on these drugs.

- Bacterial urinary infection: Unfortunately, many cats with urinary infections do not show specific **clinical signs** (i.e. the infection is 'silent') and may only show vague clinical signs such as weight loss and lethargy. A small proportion of cats with urinary infections show clinical signs of cystitis including urgency to pass urine, passing small amounts of urine very frequently and passing bloody/smelly urine. Antibiotics are needed to treat urinary tract infections – the type of antibiotic used and the duration of treatment needed will depend on the bacteria causing the infection.

Cats receiving multiple therapies can be difficult to medicate. Medicating with multiple drugs can be made easier by using empty gelatine capsules available from a vet or pharmacist. The capsule is opened, the appropriate drugs are added and then the capsule is closed again. This means that it is possible to dose a cat with two or more medicines in one go – likely to be much more popular with the cat than giving multiple pills. Giving multiple medications can increase the risk of side-effects through drug interactions which is something for you and your vet to discuss and be aware of when working out a treatment regime for your cat. If you are finding it difficult to medicate your cat ask your vet to prioritise which treatments are most important so that you can ensure that your cat is getting the most important ones everyday.

After any tablet or capsule medication is given the cat should be offered food or given a small amount of water to encourage the tablet to travel to the stomach. This is to prevent tablets or capsules from sitting in the food pipe (oesophagus) for prolonged periods where they can cause irritation and potentially serious

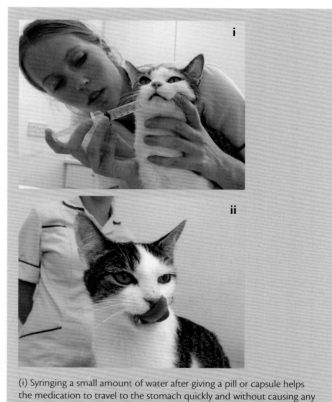

(i) Syringing a small amount of water after giving a pill or capsule helps the medication to travel to the stomach quickly and without causing any irritation to the oesophagus (food pipe). Alternatively (ii) a small amount of butter can be put on the cat's nose – licking this off also helps any pills and capsules to travel quickly to the stomach.

and long-lasting problems such as strictures (narrowing of the food pipe).

What about ACE (angiotensin converting enzyme) inhibitors such as Fortekor and kidney failure?

In addition to the special diet and the other measures outlined above, ACE inhibitors such as benazepril (trade name Fortekor, Novartis Animal Health) have recently been advocated for the treatment of cats with kidney failure. Data from clinical trials suggests that kidney failure cats receiving this therapy have a better quality of life, a better appetite, a reduction in the amount of protein they lose in their urine and may live a little longer. ACE inhibitors also lower the blood pressure and so may be prescribed as an anti-hypertensive therapy (a treatment for cats with high blood pressure). The cats that benefit most from use of an ACE inhibitor are:

- Cats losing protein into their urine (proteinuric cats)
- Cats with high blood pressure

> **Remember – not all medications mentioned in this book are veterinary approved ('licensed') for the treatment of cats and there are differences between countries as to what is available. Your vet should discuss this with you, where applicable to your cat.**

- Cats in stable renal failure (ACE inhibitors should not be used in newly diagnosed cases or in cats that are dehydrated)

Your vet should be able to advise you as to whether an ACE inhibitor is indicated in your cat.

What about calcitriol and kidney failure?

Calcitriol is a controversial treatment for cats with kidney failure – depending on where you live your vet may or may not advocate this treatment. For example, it is rarely used in the UK although quite common in certain practices in the USA.

Calcitriol is a naturally produced hormone that helps to control calcium levels in the body. It has been proposed as a treatment for cats with kidney failure as a method of normalising levels of parathyroid hormone which tend to be high in cats with this condition. Hyperparathyroidism (excessively high levels of parathyroid hormone) is common in cats with kidney failure and is thought to be harmful by exacerbating progression of their renal disease and making them feel ill (e.g. causing nausea and a poor appetite). Feeding a prescription kidney diet low in phosphate helps, as can phosphate binders, but calcitriol is also suggested by some clinicians to be useful in treating the hyperparathyroidism. Some vets feel that cats treated with calcitriol are brighter, have a better appetite, are more active and live longer. However, opinion is divided, there are some concerns over side-effects (mainly the risk of causing hypercalcaemia – an increase in blood calcium levels which can be very harmful) and there is no published hard evidence to back-up the claims made advocating the use of calcitriol in cats.

How can I give my cat the best quality and length of life possible?

For many cats, once stabilised, their care is not difficult, time-consuming or stressful and it is possible to provide a good quality of life for months or years.

Regular monitoring and vigilance for development of new problems are essential in ensuring the best care of your cat. Of all of the treatments mentioned above, kidney diets have been proven to be the most effective so all efforts should be concentrated on persuading your cat to eat these – even if it takes months to achieve this aim! However, it is always more important that your cat eats than that it eats a kidney diet so if they are not interested in the special diet, they should be offered a cat food which they will eat. Senior diets are preferable to routine cat food as these have lower levels of protein and phosphate in them.

In stable patients, check-ups should be arranged initially on a monthly basis at which time the following should be done:

■ **History taking** and **physical examination:**

  – Aim of these tests: to assess the progress of the patient since the last check-up and to look for evidence of problems associated with the kidney failure e.g. pale gums (which could indicate **anaemia**), mouth ulcers, bleeding into the eyes or retinal detachment (which could indicate high

Weight checks are vital to assess progress of cats with kidney failure. Small sets of scales, which can be housed in the vets' consulting room, are ideal for this purpose.

blood pressure), dehydration, weight loss etc. In a stable kidney failure patient, these check-ups will not always involve blood or urine samples and should not be stressful (or expensive) for you or your cat.

– Frequency of check-up required: initially monthly but in the longer term, depending on the progress of an individual patient, it may be possible to stretch out the period between check-ups. I advocate that these check-ups should be done a minimum of every 3 months in cats with kidney failure.

– Why are such regular check-ups needed in all cats?

  • A veterinary examination is the best way of detecting changes which might not be obvious at home since the carer is seeing their cat every day. For example, weight loss commonly goes unnoticed by owners (unless it becomes quite dramatic) as it is impossible to observe a small daily amount of weight loss when you are seeing your cat every day. I have seen many cats that have lost 10-20% of their body weight since the last check-up but whose owners are unaware of any change in their condition (or even think that their cat has gained weight!). Imagine how much weight loss this would be for you and hence how serious a consequence this could be for your cat!

  • A check-up every 3 months ensures that any problem, such as weight loss, is detected promptly and can therefore be addressed quickly.

  • 3 monthly check–ups maintain good contact with your vet. Good teamwork between you and your vet will lead to the best care and hence, best outcome for your cat.

■ Blood pressure measurement (where possible) and eye examination (to look for evidence of high blood pressure) should be done following a diagnosis of kidney failure. Examination of the eyes is something that can easily be done at the general check-ups and therefore can continue to be done every 3 months or whenever the cat comes in for a check-up.

  – Aim of these tests: to identify and treat high blood pressure promptly. If left untreated, high blood pressure risks serious consequences such as permanent blindness, worsening kidney disease and death.

> **A check-up every 3 months ensures that any problem is detected promptly and can therefore be addressed quickly.**

Weight loss is a very common consequence of kidney failure.

– Frequency of check-up required:

- If blood pressure is normal at the initial check then I would advocate a second check within the first two months to ensure that high blood pressure is not being overlooked. If still normal at this point then I would reduce the frequency of blood pressure check-ups to a minimum of twice a year.

- In those cats needing treatment for **systemic hypertension**, blood pressure needs to be checked more frequently – especially during the initial period of treatment. Once blood pressure is stable subsequent check-ups can be done less frequently. This is something that I do gradually according to the patient – for example reducing the frequency of blood pressure checks to a minimum of once every 3-4 months if very stable.

– Why are such regular check-ups needed in all cats? **Systemic hypertension** is often referred to as the 'silent killer' – blood pressure checks ensure that high blood pressure is identified quickly helping to prevent development of consequences associated with this condition.

■ Repeat laboratory tests:

– Aim of these tests:

- To check whether treatment for complications of the kidney disease (e.g. **hyperphosphataemia**) has been successful or whether it needs adjusting

- To check whether new complications of the kidney failure have appeared

- To monitor progression of the kidney disease itself

– Frequency of check-up required:

- As indicated by the results of a history and **physical examination** – for example if your vet is suspicious of **anaemia** (for example if your cat's gums appear very pale) then a **haematology** profile may be indicated to assess the numbers of red blood cells and haemoglobin content.

- Once a patient is stable, repeat blood and urine tests are generally indicated every 6 months.

Cats should be returned for check-ups sooner if you have any concerns. Specific causes for concern include:

■ Sudden deterioration or loss of vision

■ Loss of appetite which persists for more than 24 hours

■ Severe weakness – e.g. unable to raise the head ('ventroflexion of the neck') which may indicate **hypokalaemia**.

■ Vomiting more frequently

■ Severe lethargy/listlessness

Are routine vaccinations and worming still needed in cats with kidney failure?

Cats with stable and well managed kidney failure still benefit from routine preventative health care such as vaccination. All illnesses – including kidney failure – reduce a cat's ability to fight infections so they will be more vulnerable to severe illness if they contract an infection. Visits to a veterinary practice can be stressful (which can lower immunity) and risk contact with infectious agents.

As always, follow your vet's advice on what is most appropriate for your cat. For example, an indoor-only cat that has no access to hunting or fleas does not generally need to be de-wormed and de-fleaed.

What is the prognosis (long-term outlook) for cats with kidney failure?

The long-term outlook for cats with kidney failure is very variable, ranging from a few weeks to many years following diagnosis. Kidney failure is always considered to be a progressive disease – i.e. it will get worse with time although the rate of progression varies between individual cats.

Prognosis is dependent upon the cause of the disease, the rate of worsening of disease, concurrent medical problems and the severity of the consequences of the kidney disease. Owner and veterinary monitoring of the affected cat helps to assess the severity of the disease and its rate of progression which ensures that the cat receives all of the treatments it needs to help maintain good health. Care of affected cats at home can be very rewarding and is helpful in ensuring that the cat has the best quality of life for as long as possible.

Morgan, a cat with kidney failure and a happy outcome!

Morgan, a part-Persian cat, was presented to me as a referral patient in December 2004 when she had just turned four years old. She had been ill for two months and her main clinical signs were a poor appetite, nausea, vomiting, weight loss and recurrent episodes of dehydration which required hospitalisation to treat.

Severe kidney failure was diagnosed and Morgan was also found to be suffering from almost all of the consequences of kidney disease. She had:

- A very severe azotaemia with ten times the normal amount of urea and creatinine in her blood (urea 90 mmol/l, creatinine 1800 μmol/l)

- Severe acidosis

- Severe hyperphosphataemia

- Anaemia

- Dehydration

Morgan was hospitalised for several days, during which time we successfully corrected most of these problems and she was able to return home eating and bright.

For almost three years, home management has been successful in preventing re-hospitalisation. Morgan has daily subcutaneous fluids at home and a cocktail of additional therapies (including iron, anti-sickness drugs, phosphate binders, vitamins and appetite stimulants). All of her treatments can be given in one empty gelatine capsule which means that medication is not stressful for her (or her owner!) and takes less than five minutes a day to administer. She has gained weight, is bright and active and has an excellent quality of life in spite of her severe kidney disease.

(i) Morgan at the time of first presentation

(ii) Back home when stable.

A good relationship with your vet is vital to the care and wellbeing of your cat with kidney failure. It is important therefore that you feel able to discuss all of your concerns openly. Your vet is in the best position to advise you regarding specific questions on treatment and **prognosis** – for example whether or not your cat could benefit from treatment with subcutaneous fluids or whether certain drugs are indicated. You should feel able to ask your vet any questions and they should be able to explain things to you clearly in a way you can understand.

If you feel that the relationship you have with your vet is not answering your concerns then you can ask to see another vet within the practice, or look for another practice. Do not feel uncomfortable if you want to do this – your vet should not mind and it is within your rights to choose the vet you feel is best able to look after your cat. It is always worthwhile asking if there is anyone in the practice who is particularly interested in cat medicine. The UK cat charity, the Feline Advisory Bureau, has a list of UK vet practices that are members of the charity (see **http://www.fabcats.org/owners/choosing_a_vet/practice_ members1.php**) which is a good indication of enthusiasm and knowledge in feline medicine. A number of feline-only practices also exist and you may be fortunate in finding one of these in your area.

Veterinary surgeons specialising in feline medicine can be contacted by your vet for further advice, if needed, or referral to a specialist can be arranged.

In order for your vet to be able to provide the level of care you are looking for with your cat, they will need to understand things from your perspective. For example:

■ Will you be able to medicate your cat at home or is this out of the question (for example because your cat is very feisty or because you have severe arthritis in your fingers)? Will giving some medications be possible (e.g. dietary treatment) but others not possible (e.g. tablets)?

■ What are your expectations for your cat? For example, would you prefer minimum intervention accepting a potentially shorter time with your cat or are you keen for your cat to have every possible medical treatment?

■ Are finances limited in which case certain treatments may be too expensive? Your vet will be able to advise you on the likely cost of treating your cat.

■ Are there any particular treatments which you object to being used in your cat?

Once both of you know what your expectations are then it should be possible to jointly work out a treatment plan that is appropriate for your cat. It is important to remember that all treatment plans can be modified – at any time – and that anything you agree to can be changed, if needed, in the future.

Knowing when to say 'goodbye'

How long has my cat got before he/she dies or needs putting to sleep (euthanasia)?

This is an impossible question for me to answer as it varies enormously from cat to cat. Lots of cats can live a normal quality of life for some years after a diagnosis of kidney failure has been made. Sadly some die or need to be put to sleep (euthanased) soon after the diagnosis is made. Your vet is in the best position to advise on your own cat and its likely **prognosis**.

Will I know when it's time to say goodbye to my cat and let him/her go?

It is very rare for an elderly sick cat to die painlessly in their sleep – much though most owners would wish this to happen. Death tends to be a slow and distressing process and it is far kinder to intervene and ask a vet to put your cat to sleep (euthanase it) when the time has come than let your cat suffer a prolonged and possibly painful death. It is therefore a sad inevitability that one day you are likely to have to decide that your cat needs putting to sleep. For many owners the thought of making this decision is painful and worrying. Most owners feel that their cat should be put to sleep once their quality of life has deteriorated and there is no veterinary treatment that can help to improve this. Your vet should be able to support and guide you in making this decision – if you are at all worried then consult them for advice.

Quality of life is not easy to judge but guidelines include:

■ Behaviour:

  a) Is your cat still behaving in its normal way – following its usual routines and activities (e.g. spending the same amount of time grooming)? Is your cat interacting with you as normal?

  b) OR, has your cat become withdrawn and quiet, not interested in going outside (if normally allowed out) or in interacting with you and other animals in the home?

■ Appetite:

  a) Is your cat still interested in food?

  b) OR, has their appetite disappeared and getting them to eat has become a struggle?

■ Toileting behaviour:

  a) Is your cat still passing urine and faeces in the litter tray (or outside in the garden) as is normal for them?

  b) OR, has your cat started to pass urine and faeces in other places (such as on their bed or on your carpets and flooring)?

- Vocalisation:

  a) Is your cat as chatty as normal?

  b) OR, has there been a change in the amount of vocalisation (increase or decrease) or the sound that your cat makes when miaowing?

- Pain or distress:

  a) Does your cat seem happy and comfortable?

  b) OR, have you seen any sign of pain or discomfort – for example signs of fear or aggression when being handled or sitting in the same place for hours with a glazed expression?

- Signs of illness:

  a) Is your cat free of signs of illness?

  b) OR, is it suffering from signs of illness such as vomiting, weight loss or constipation?

If you answer b) to any of the above questions then you should consult your vet for advice on whether there are any treatments that can help your cat to regain its quality of life. If there are, you need to consider whether to give these treatments a try before making any final decisions.

What does euthanasia involve?

For most veterinary surgeons, euthanasia involves giving an overdose injection of a barbiturate anaesthetic agent intravenously, usually into a vein in the front leg. Once the injection is started, the cat will lose consciousness within a few seconds and the heart should stop within a few minutes. Occasionally, the veins of the front leg can be very fragile and difficult to access so alternative injection sites need to be used – these include the kidneys and the liver. In any case, the process should be quick and painless.

Although the majority of cats are put to sleep at a veterinary practice, most vets will be happy to come to an owner's home to do this, if desired.

What happens to my cat's body after they die or are euthanased (put to sleep)?

In general the options will be:

- Burying your cat's body at home

- Asking your vet to arrange cremation of your cat's body. If desired, you can ask for an individual cremation to be performed and for the ashes to be returned to you.

Your vet will be able to discuss these options with you. It is worthwhile considering how you would like your cat to be put to sleep (should the need arise) and what you would like to happen to their body while your cat is still well. This will save you the added distress of these decisions when your cat dies.

How to cope with losing your cat

Is there support available for me in my grief?

Losing a beloved cat is always going to be a traumatic and distressing experience and you are likely to go through several acknowledged stages of grief. These include denial, anger, guilt, hopelessness/depression and finally acceptance. Most people experience at least two of these stages. Carers of cats with terminal illnesses such as kidney failure may start to go through this process as soon as the diagnosis is made. Where this is the case, a further stage of grief – 'bargaining' – may also be experienced where an owner is keen for their cat to live to a certain point (for example, please let them live through Christmas so we can have this time together).

Hopefully you will have friends and family that will be able to provide some support to you throughout this period. If you don't, then consider talking to the vets or nurses at your veterinary practice, your doctor or a priest – all of whom should be able to offer support. There may be local support groups available (your veterinary practice should know about these) and there is also a UK helpline available for dedicated pet bereavement counselling, the Pet Bereavement Support Service (PBSS): 0800 096 6606 open from 8.30am to 8.30pm daily. All calls are free and confidential. The PBSS also offers an e-mail support service: pbssmail@bluecross.org.uk

More information on this service is available on: http://www.bluecross.org.uk/web/site/AboutUs/PetBereavement/ContactingPBSS.asp

What about my other cat/s – are they likely to grieve?

Yes, it is possible. As with people, cats can show grief at the loss of a companion. The behaviour of a cat following the loss of a house-mate is very variable and unpredictable. Some cats seem completely unaffected by the loss, some appear happier once they are on their own whilst others may show signs of grief such as sleeping less, not eating, appearing to look for their lost companion and vocalising more or losing all interest in life.

This process can affect cats (and other animals) for up to a year following their loss. In most cases, signs of grief will disappear within 6 months. You can help affected cats in the following ways:

- Keep routines in the home the same

- If your cat has lost its appetite then try hand-feeding food that has been slightly warmed (to just below body temperature). Consult your vet if your cat has not eaten for three or more days. A complete loss of appetite can cause a potentially fatal liver disease called hepatic lipidosis.

■ Provide reassurance to your cat by spending more time with them, grooming them, talking to them and playing with them.

■ Don't immediately get a new cat. Although some cats will crave the company of a new companion, many cats will be more upset and distressed if a new cat is introduced too soon. Many cats prefer to be in single cat households and it is impossible to predict what they will feel about a newcomer. So, if your cat seems happy after the loss of a house-mate I would not get another cat. If, on the other hand, you are keen to expand the home or feel that your cat is 'lonely' then I would advise waiting for at least a couple of months before considering introducing a new cat.

More information on feline bereavement is available on the FAB website: http://www.fabcats.org/owners/euthanasia/bereavement.html. The FAB also has advice on introducing a new cat which could be helpful once a decision has been made to get another cat: http://www.fabcats.org/behaviour/introducing/info.html

Useful websites

Several websites have been mentioned in this publication and you might find these interesting to look at:

General cat advice

The Feline Advisory Bureau http://www.fabcats.org

The Blue Cross http://www.bluecross.org.uk/web/site/home/home.asp

Cats Protection http://www.cats.org.uk/

The Royal Society for the Prevention of Cruelty to Animals http://www.rspca.org.uk/

The Cat Group http://www.fabcats.org/cat_group/index.html

American Association of Feline Practitioners http://www.aafponline.org/

Choosing a veterinary practice

http://www.fabcats.org/owners/choosing_a_vet/practice_members1.php

Information on kidney disease

http://www.iris-kidney.com

http://www.felinecrf.com/index.htm

http://www.felinecrf.org/

Giving subcutaneous fluids to your cat

http://www.fabcats.org/owners/kidney/subcutaneous/info.html

Bereavement support

http://www.bluecross.org.uk/web/site/AboutUs/PetBereavement/ContactingPBSS.asp
http://www.fabcats.org/owners/euthanasia/bereavement.html

Introducing a new cat to the home

http://www.fabcats.org/behaviour/introducing/info.html

Glossary of terms used by vets

Term (pronunciation – emphasised syllables in bold)	Definition
Acidosis (ass-id-**oh**-sis)	The blood is more acidic than normal. This is one potential consequence of kidney failure and can make affected cats lose their appetite, feel nauseous and generally off colour.
Acute renal failure – ARF (ack-**you**-t **ree**-nal **fay**-lure)	Sudden loss of kidney function which can be caused by one or more of the following: ■ Reduced blood supply to the kidneys (so called pre-renal ARF). Causes include heart failure and dehydration. ■ Damage to the kidneys themselves (renal or intrinsic ARF). Causes include poisoning e.g. antifreeze (ethylene glycol), eating lilies. ■ Failure of urine excretion due to a blockage in the urethra (tube from the bladder to the outside) or rupture of the bladder. This is called post-renal ARF. Although many causes of ARF are fully treatable (and the kidney damage can be reversed), if severe and untreated, ARF can progress to CRF.
Anaemia (a-**neem**-ee-a)	A reduction in the numbers of red blood cells in the circulation. Red blood cells (also known as erythrocytes) carry oxygen to the tissues of the body so anaemic cats will often be weak and listless. Anaemias are subdivided into: ■ Regenerative anaemias: ones in which the bone marrow (which manufactures red blood cells) is responding to the anaemia and trying to correct this ■ Non-regenerative anaemias: ones in which the bone marrow response (ability to produce more new erythrocytes) is insufficient or absent.
Anaesthesia (ann-ess-**thee**-zee-ya)	Providing a state of unconsciousness, muscle relaxation and loss of pain sensation using certain drugs (usually a combination of intravenously and by gas inhalation).

Term (pronunciation – emphasised syllables in bold)	Definition
Anorexia (an-or-**ex**-ee-a)	Complete loss of appetite.
Ascites (ass-**eye**-teez)	Accumulation of fluid in the abdominal cavity (the space around all of the abdominal organs).
Azotaemia (ay-zo-**teem**-ee-a)	Accumulation of protein breakdown products such as urea and creatinine in the blood. Measurement of urea and creatinine levels is used to diagnose kidney failure (see 'How is kidney failure diagnosed?').
Biochemistry (bi-oh-**kem**-iss-tree)	Refers to blood tests of organ function (e.g. urea and creatinine), blood salt levels and protein levels.
Biopsy (**bi**-op-see)	Collection and laboratory analysis of a sample of tissue e.g. kidney biopsy.
Calcaemia (cal-**seem**-ee-a)	Referring to levels of calcium in the blood stream e.g. hypocalcaemia refers to sub-normal calcium levels.
Chronic interstitial nephritis (**kronn**-ick inter-**stish**-all neff-**rye**-tiss)	See **nephritis**.
Chronic renal failure – CRF (**kronn**-ick **ree**-nal **fay**-lure)	Inadequate kidney function which has been present for at least 2 weeks. This is considered to be a progressive condition – it will get worse with time – although the speed of progression is variable.

Term (pronunciation – emphasised syllables in bold)	Definition
Clinical examination	Examination of body systems by a veterinary surgeon or nurse. Typically this includes listening to the chest, opening the mouth and feeling the tummy.
Clinical signs	The term used to describe what we would call our 'symptoms' if we were the cat e.g. sickness, loss of appetite.
Cystitis (sist-**eye**-tiss)	Inflammation of the urinary bladder (where urine is stored before urination). One cause would be a bacterial infection of the urine.
Cystocentesis (siss-toe-sen-**tee**-siss)	Technique of urine collection using a needle and syringe. The needle is passed through the skin and into the bladder from which urine is collected.
Electrolyte (ell-**eck**-troe-lite)	Blood salt – the most important blood salts in cats with kidney failure are sodium, potassium, calcium and phosphate.
Erythropoietin (e-rith-row-po-**eat**-in)	A hormone produced by the kidneys which stimulates production of red blood cells by the bone marrow. A lack of erythropoietin is one cause of the anaemia (low red blood cell numbers) which can be seen in cats with kidney failure.
Euthanasia (youth-an-**ay**-zee-a)	Also referred to as 'putting to sleep' this is the term used when a vet ends a cat's life. This is usually done by giving an overdose of barbiturate anaesthetic into a vein – the cat dies within seconds of the injection being given.
Glomerulonephropathy (glom-**air**-you-low-neff-**rop**-ath-ee)	Disease affecting the glomerulus and often causing loss of protein from the bloodstream into the urine.

Term (*pronunciation – emphasised syllables in bold*)	Definition
Glomerulus (*glom-**air**-you-luss*)	The small mass of blood vessels encased in the Bowmans capsule of the nephron. Blood in the glomerular capillaries is filtered here to produce urine which passes through the kidney tubules (being modified as it goes) to the renal pelvis.
Haematology (*heem-a-**tol**-a-gee*)	Laboratory test assessing the blood count, numbers and types of white blood cells and platelets.
History taking	This is the process by which your vet gathers information on your cat and all of its problems (clinical signs).
Hyper- (*high-purr*)	Increased e.g. hyperphosphataemia: increased blood phosphate levels.
Hypo- (*high-poe*)	Reduced e.g. hypokalaemia: low levels of potassium in the blood; hypoproteinaemia: low levels of protein in the blood.
Inappetence (*inn-**app**-ett-en-s*)	Poor appetite.
Inflammation (*inn-fla-**may**-shun*)	A response of injured or damaged cells which helps to wall off the problem, eliminate infectious substances (for example) and restore healthy tissue. The classic signs of inflammation are: ■ Heat ■ Pain ■ Redness ■ Swelling ■ Loss of function.

Term (pronunciation – emphasised syllables in bold)	Definition
Inflammatory (inn-**flam**-at-tory)	Pertaining to inflammation.
Kalaemia (cal-**eem**-ee-a)	Referring to levels of potassium in the blood stream e.g. hypokalaemia refers to sub-normal potassium levels.
Natraemia (nat-**reem**-ee-a)	Referring to levels of sodium in the blood stream e.g. hyponatraemia refers to sub-normal sodium levels.
Nephritis (neff-**rye**-tiss)	Inflammatory process present within the kidney/s. This term can be further qualified according to the location of the inflammation – for example: ■ Pyelonephritis: inflammation of the kidney and renal pelvis ■ Chronic interstitial nephritis (CIN): inflammation of the kidney including the tissues between the nephrons. CIN is commonly diagnosed in cats with renal failure and often represents an end-stage of many different types of kidney disease. ■ Glomerulonephritis: inflammation of the kidney and glomerulus.
Nephron (**neff**-ron)	The functional unit of the kidney: the nephron is a tubule which produces urine and carries it to the renal pelvis. Each normal feline kidney contains about 200,000 nephrons.
Nephropathy (neff-**rop**-ath-ee)	Abnormal development or disease causing destruction of the kidney.
Nephrosis (neff-**row**-siss)	Degeneration of the kidney tissue e.g. following exposure to a toxic substance.

Term (pronunciation – emphasised syllables in bold)	Definition
Nephrotic syndrome (neff-**rot**-ic sin-dr-oh-m)	The term used specifically to describe patients with such severe protein loss from the kidneys that their blood protein levels are sub-normal (hypoproteinaemia) and the cat is suffering from clinical signs as a consequence of this (e.g. ascites: fluid development within the abdomen).
Oedema (e-**deem**-a)	The accumulation of excessive amounts of watery fluid in the cells or spaces between the cells. This can lead to puffiness of the skin and is a potential consequence of hypoproteinaemia.
Pathologist (pa-**tholl**-oj-iss-t)	A specialist in pathology who is able to diagnose the cause and/or type of disease by examining biopsy samples.
Pathology (pa-**tholl**-oj-ee)	The study of disease.
Phosphataemia (foss-fa-**teem**-ee-a)	Referring to levels of phosphate in the blood stream e.g. hypophosphataemia refers to sub-normal phosphate levels.
Physical examination	Examination of body systems by a veterinary surgeon or nurse. Typically this includes listening to the chest, opening the mouth and feeling the tummy.
Pica (**pee**-ka)	An abnormal appetite – for example eating cat litter, soil, licking concrete. Often associated with anaemia in cats.
Pleural fluid (ploor-all floo-id)	Accumulation of fluid in the chest space around the lungs.
Polydipsia (polly-**dip**-see-a)	An increased thirst.

Term (pronunciation – emphasised syllables in bold)	Definition
Polyuria (polly-**you**-ree-a)	Increased volume of urine produced (usually noticed as the cat is passing normal volumes of urine more frequently).
Prognosis (prog-**no**-siss)	A forecast of the likely long-term outlook for a cat with a given condition/s.
Proteinaemia (pro-teen-**eem**-ee-a)	Referring to levels of protein in the bloodstream therefore hypoproteinaemia refers to abnormally low levels of protein in the bloodstream.
Proteinuria (pro-teen-**you**-ree-a)	Abnormally high levels of protein in the urine (normally there should be very little protein present in the urine). Causes include glomerulonephropathy.
Proteinuric (pro-teen-**you**-ric)	Suffering from proteinuria.
Pyelitis (pie-ell-**eye**-tiss)	Inflammation of the renal pelvis.
Radiograph (**ray**-dee-oh-gr-ah-ff)	X-ray.
Refractometer (ree-frack-**tom**-eat-er)	An instrument that can measure the concentration of urine.
Renal (**ree**-nal)	Relating to the kidney/s.

Term (pronunciation – emphasised syllables in bold)	Definition
Renal pelvis (**ree**-nal **pel**-viss)	The location where urine produced by the nephrons accumulates. From here, urine is taken to the bladder in the ureters.
Sedation (sed-**ay**-shun)	Providing a state of calm and muscle relaxation using drugs. The cat is still conscious but, depending on the drugs used, may appear quite sleepy.
Systemic hypertension (siss-**tem**-ic **high**-purr-ten-shun)	An increase in the blood pressure of the systemic blood supply (the blood supply to all of the body except the lungs).
Toxin	Poisonous. A nephrotoxin is poisonous to the kidneys.
Trauma	Injury or wound.
Uraemic syndrome (you-**reem**-ic sin-dr-oh-m)	This term is used to describe the clinical signs which are seen in cats with kidney failure. Examples would include gastritis (inflammation of the stomach lining causing vomiting and poor appetite), systemic hypertension (high blood pressure) and metabolic acidosis (blood more acidic than it should be).
Ureter (**you**-ree-tur)	Small tubes which take urine from each kidney to the bladder.
Urethra (you-**ree**-thr-a)	Tube which carries urine from the bladder to the outside of the body.
Urinalysis (you-rin-**ally**-siss)	Laboratory analysis of a urine sample e.g. number of cells, acidity, protein levels.
Urine protein to creatinine (cree-**a**-tin-in) **ratio: UPC or PCR test**	A laboratory test which quantifies the severity of proteinuria. Ratios greater than 0.4 are currently considered to be abnormally high.

Converting SI units to Conventional units and vice versa

Parameter	To convert Conventional to SI multiply by...	To convert SI to Conventional multiply by...
Urea	0.357	2.8
Creatinine	88.4	0.0113
Phosphate	0.323	3.1
Potassium	1	1
Sodium	1	1
Calcium	0.25	4
Albumin	10	0.1
Total protein	10	0.1
Bicarbonate	1	1
Packed cell volume (PCV) or haematocrit	0.01	100
Haemoglobin (Hb)	10	0.1